THE LEGEND OF TUTANKHAMUN

Sally Morgan
James Weston Lewis

wren
&rook

'May'st thou spend millions of years,
thou lover of Thebes, sitting with
thy face to the north wind and thine
eyes beholding happiness.'

Inscription on Tutankhamun's Wishing Cup

CONTENTS

A GIFT FROM THE GODS

Long, long ago, the great kingdom of ancient Egypt stretched along the river Nile in an area now known as Northeast Africa. The kings of this rich and prosperous land were called pharaohs. They lived in magnificent palaces filled with tapestries, sculptures and priceless treasures. Outside were beautiful gardens, with exotic flowers, fruit trees, ponds and walkways.

The pharaoh was all-powerful and the people, from the lowliest slave to the highest noble, strove to satisfy his every wish. They idolised their ruler and believed that when he died he would be transported to the afterlife where he would live for ever among the gods.

The people of these ancient times believed that their gods controlled everything, from daily family life to the setting of the sun and the rising of the moon, and that their rich and fertile land and fresh, clean water was their reward for honouring their gods.

It was into this world around 1341 BCE that a baby boy was born, who would become the most famous pharaoh in history. This is his story.

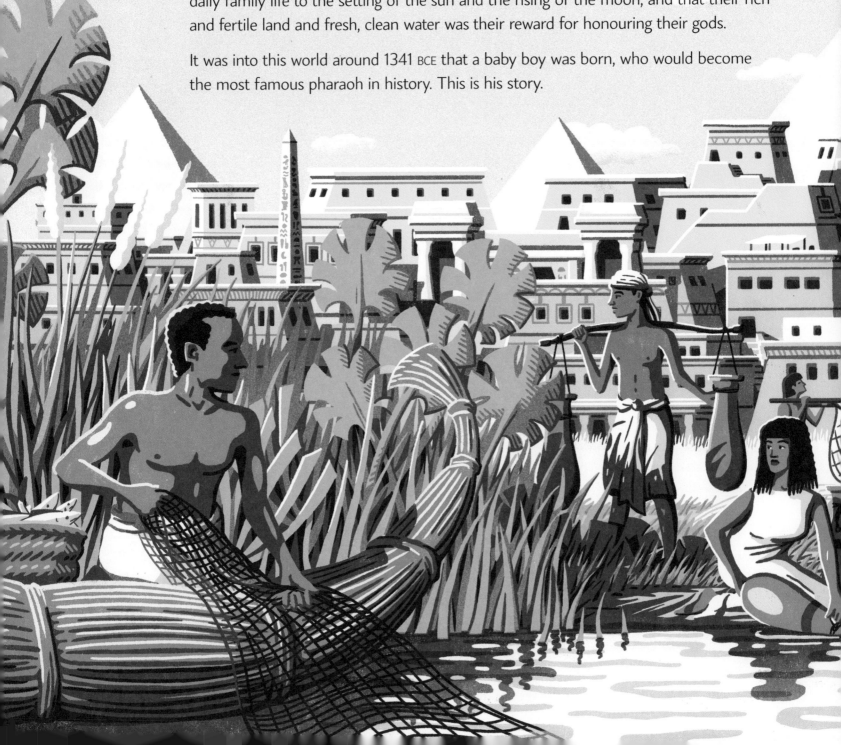

ATEN

God of the Sun disk

AMUN

God of the Sun

ANUBIS

God of the dead and mummification

SOBEK

God of the Nile

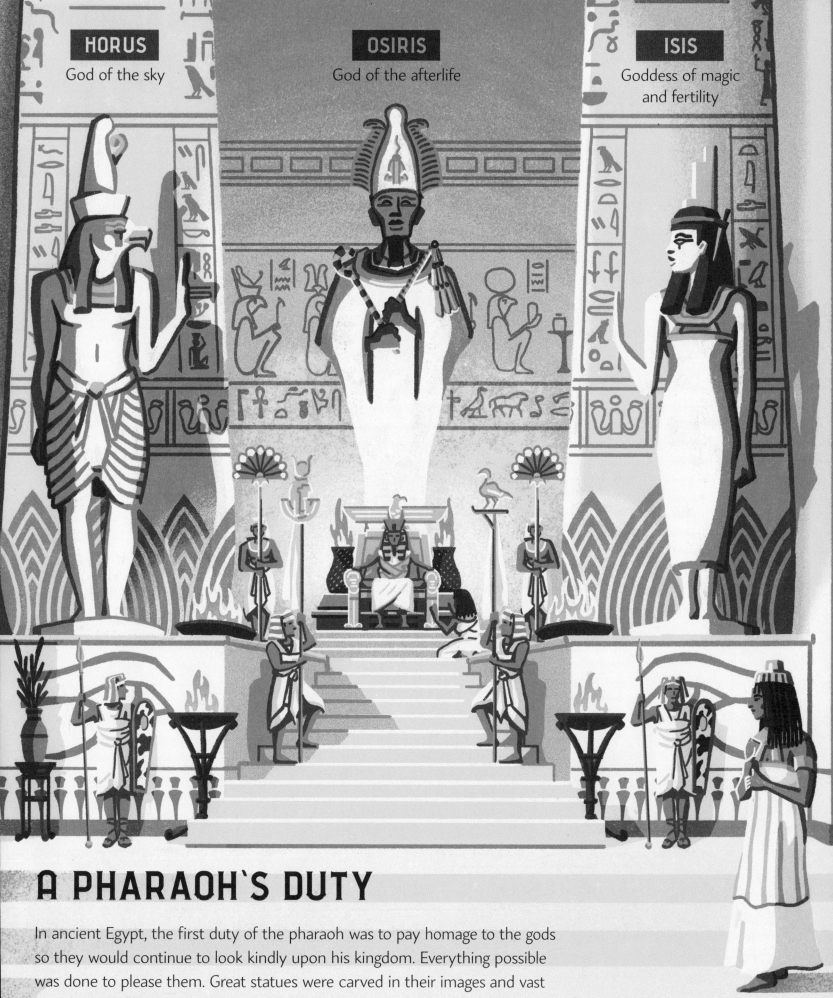

HORUS
God of the sky

OSIRIS
God of the afterlife

ISIS
Goddess of magic and fertility

A PHARAOH'S DUTY

In ancient Egypt, the first duty of the pharaoh was to pay homage to the gods so they would continue to look kindly upon his kingdom. Everything possible was done to please them. Great statues were carved in their images and vast temples built for their worship.

The pharaoh was also responsible for keeping peace and harmony throughout his lands, looking after nature and making sure his people were protected and well cared for.

ONE TRUE GOD

About the year 1353 BCE, a period of unhappiness and unrest came to this bountiful land. A new pharaoh, Amenhotep IV, had come to the throne and introduced a new law. He decreed that it was forbidden to worship any god but Aten – the god of the Sun disk – and ordered that all images, statues and scriptures representing the other gods be destroyed.

Amenhotep told his people that he was the earthly son of Aten. He said Aten had visited him to reveal that he was the one and only true god. Whether they believed him or not, there was nothing the people of Egypt could do. Amenhotep was their ruler and the pharaoh's word must be obeyed. But many secretly held on to their beliefs and harboured hatred in their hearts for their new ruler.

THE BOY KING

In honour of his one chosen god, Amenhotep changed his name to Akhenaten, meaning 'useful for Aten', and ordered the building of a new capital city to be called Akhetaten. It was here he ruled side by side with his great royal wife, the powerful Queen Nefertiti, famed for her beauty. Nefertiti gave birth to six princesses, but produced no son and heir. However, pharaohs had several wives, and in 1341 BCE, a long-awaited baby boy was born to one of the pharaoh's senior wives, Kiya. The child was named Tutankaten, which meant 'living image of Aten'.

The young prince was slender and tall for his age, but he had fragile bones and a club foot which made it painful to walk. However, he was clever and brave and refused to let his disabilities hold him back. He learned to ride a chariot and shoot with a bow and arrow, and studied hard at the Princes' School where he was taught reading, writing, maths, science, and all about the history of his land and beyond. His skills and knowledge proved vital because when his father died, the young Tutankhaten became king of all Egypt in 1333 BCE, at the age of eight!

As the young pharaoh sat on his magnificent, golden throne in the great riverside palace at Akhetaten, he must have felt both proud and afraid. How could he, a young boy, command such a great kingdom?

Fortunately he had an advisor, known as a vizier, to guide him. His name was Ay.

THE BOLD YOUNG KING

The year he was crowned, Tutankaten was married to his half-sister, Princess Ankhesenpaaten. Even though they were just children, they had to leave their games behind and begin to take up the roles and duties of a king and queen.

Tutankaten grew into a bold young man. He loved hunting and training for battle, and started taking more interest in the affairs of his land. He soon sensed the growing unhappiness among his people and sought advice from his vizier, Ay…

THE RETURN OF THE GODS

Tutankaten listened to Ay describe how, when he was vizier to Tutankaten's father, he saw the way the old pharaoh puffed himself up, calling himself and his wife Nefertiti gods. He spoke of the great fortune the pharaoh had spent on making his palace and city ever more magnificent, and that he had cared very little about what was going on beyond his royal surroundings. Things had been very different, Ay told the young king, when the great god Amun ruled, together with Osiris, Sobek, Horus and all the other gods who had once looked after Egypt and protected its people.

Tutankaten made a decision. He changed his name to Tutankhamun, 'living image of Amun', and ordered his father's temples to Aten be torn down and glorious new temples to the old gods built in their place. He moved his court back to the religious capital of Thebes. The people rejoiced!

Then, tragedy struck. When he was only 19 years old, Tutankhamun died. Nobody knew why. Some thought it was an illness, some thought it was because of an infected wound, some even thought he had been murdered. The one thing they did know was that their beloved young king had brought back their former gods, and with them the start of a new period of peace, harmony and prosperity.

Great care was taken to prepare Tutankhamun's body for the afterlife. His organs were removed, but his heart was left inside to be weighed by the gods against 'the feather of truth'. If it was lighter, his heart was pure and he would be allowed to enter the afterlife. The priests preparing his body had no doubts that their cherished ruler would pass the test and be welcomed into the afterlife to live for ever among the gods.

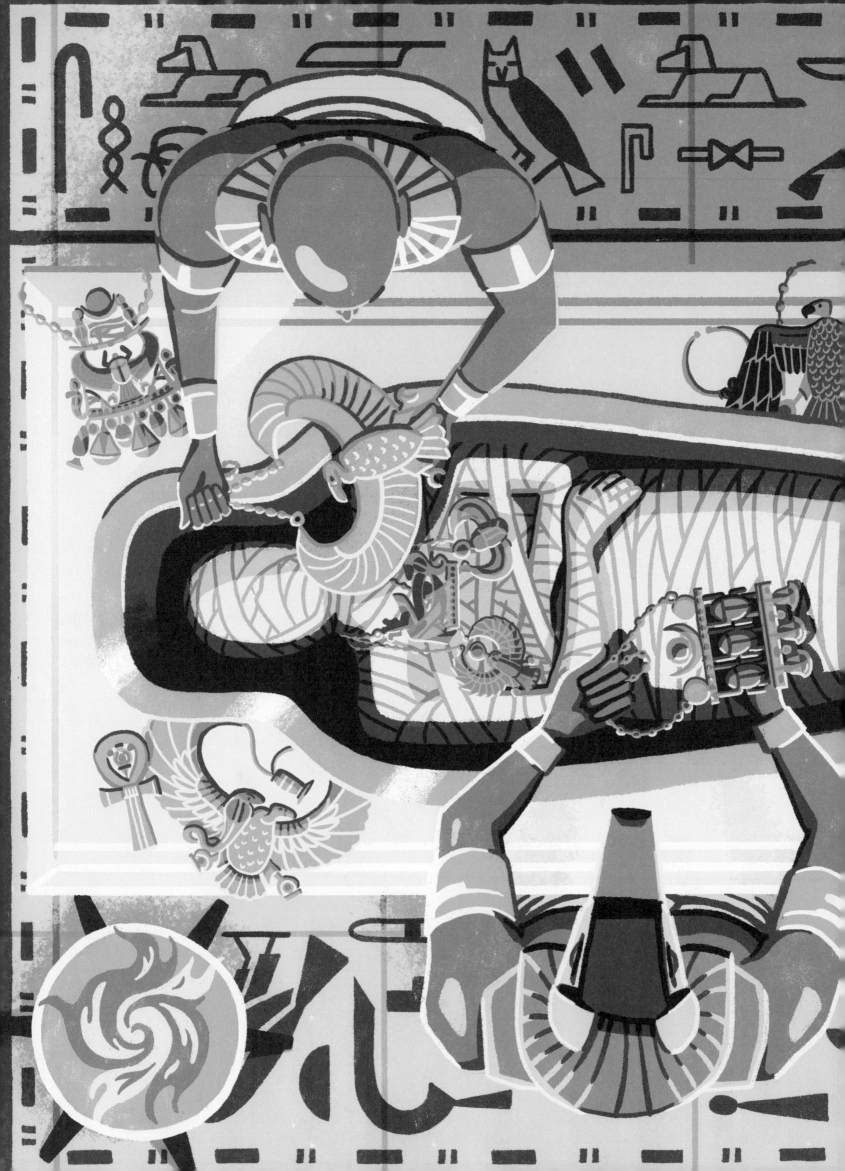

A ROYAL BURIAL

After his organs had been removed, Tutankhamun's body was dried out using a salt called natron during a process known as mummification.

His mummy was then wrapped in strips of the finest linen, and amulets and charms were placed between the layers to protect him on his way to the afterlife.

A magnificent mask of gold, inset with brilliant blue lapis lazuli stones, was made in the image of the young pharaoh and placed over his face.

His mummy was then put inside a coffin of solid gold which nestled inside two jewelled caskets. The caskets were placed inside another coffin made of stone, called a sarcophagus, and encased by four golden boxes called shrines, each one fastened with a seal.

THE LONGEST JOURNEY

Tutankhamun's sarcophagus was placed in his tomb, which was filled with everything a young pharaoh might need to help him on his journey to the afterlife.

MORE THAN 30 JARS OF WINE

14 WRITING PALETTES

2 TRUMPETS

2 JARS OF HONEY

6 CHARIOTS

6 CHAIRS

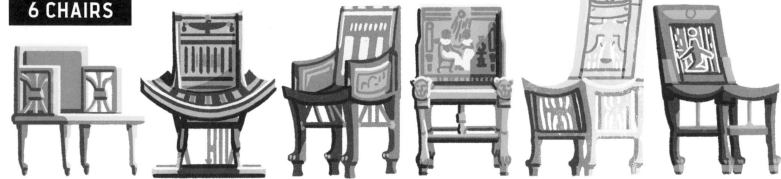

35 MODEL BOATS

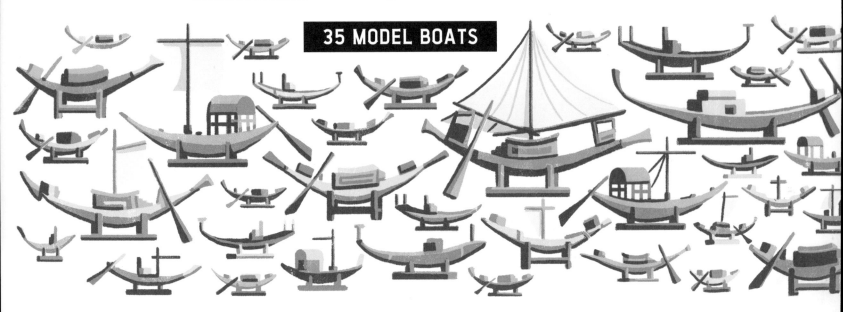

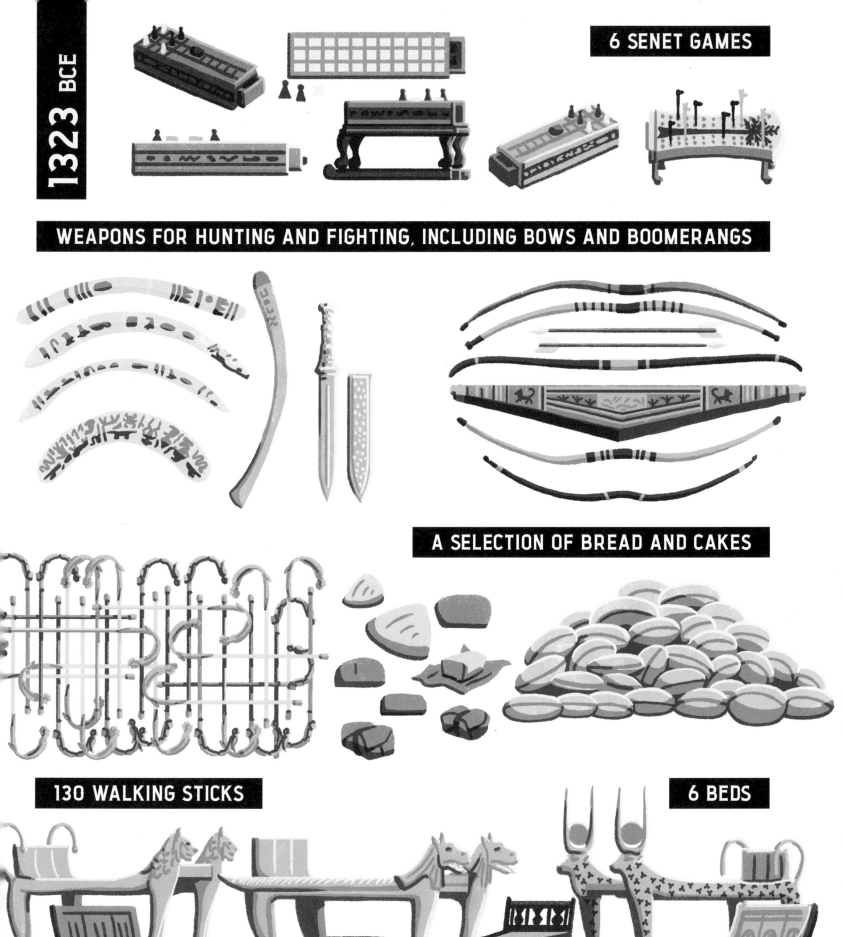

1323 BCE

6 SENET GAMES

WEAPONS FOR HUNTING AND FIGHTING, INCLUDING BOWS AND BOOMERANGS

A SELECTION OF BREAD AND CAKES

130 WALKING STICKS

6 BEDS

The tomb was then sealed with the mark of the guards of the royal burial ground.

THE LONGEST WAIT

There Tutankhamun lay for four years, until 1319 BCE, when his tomb was disturbed twice by thieves. Both times the thieves were caught, some of their loot carelessly put back, and the entrance resealed and buried.

Despite Tutankhamun having restored Egypt's gods, the pharaohs that followed were determined to erase all memory of Tutankhamun's father, Akhenaten. To do this, inscriptions bearing his, or any member of his family's name, were scrubbed out, and so the name of Tutankhamun and the location of his final resting place were forgotten. Workers on the tomb of the pharaoh Rameses VI unknowingly built their huts right over Tutankhamun's tomb, burying the doorway and the secrets that lay beyond.

As the desert sands shifted and swirled above Tutankhamun's tomb, the world moved on. Great civilizations rose and fell, and much of what is known today about the pharaohs and their great empire was lost.

THE WRITING ON THE RUINS

The secrets of the pharaohs lay lost for thousands of years. Then in 1799 CE, soldiers from the French army were in a town called Rosetta, in Egypt, rebuilding a fort, when one of the officers, Lieutenant Bouchard, noticed an unusual stone that had fallen from a wall. As he stepped closer he saw that the stone was covered with strange writing. His heart began to beat faster.

He knew at once that this was something remarkable! What he had found was a stela, a stone slab from the ancient world used to make announcements or record important events.

The stela was written in three different scripts: Greek, hieratic and hieroglyphics, the picture writing of the ancient Egyptians. No one had been able to understand hieroglyphics or hieratic before, but they could understand Greek. The most exciting thing of all was that the Greek text revealed that all three scripts were saying the same thing! Here at last was the key to understanding the written language of the ancient Egyptians. The secrets of the pharaohs were to be unlocked!

Hidden behind towering cliffs near the city of Thebes lay a place of eerie, barren beauty. This was the Valley of the Kings, the sacred burial grounds of the pharaohs. Early in the twentieth century, an American called Theodore M. Davis discovered over 30 tombs buried deep in its rocks. He unearthed numerous treasures, but many of the tombs had been robbed; in 1914 he gave up his search, believing there were no more to be found.

But there was someone who would prove him wrong, and that story began almost 40 years before, near a small village called Didlington in Norfolk, England.

THE DOORWAY TO AN ANCIENT WORLD

In the early 1880s, in an old stately home in England, a little boy called Howard Carter opened a door to discover a room full of wonder and magic. His eyes grew wide with excitement. Inside were treasures from another world: statues of pharaohs from ancient Egypt, and of the gods that ruled them, and gorgeously illustrated scrolls containing spells written in a strange and beautiful text. They belonged to the collector William Amherst, who had employed Carter's artist father to work on some paintings.

Carter grew up to become a talented artist himself, and when the British Museum was looking for someone to travel to Egypt to sketch for them, William Amherst suggested him for the post. Ever since that wondrous visit to Amherst's house, Carter had harboured a passion for Egypt and its treasures, and at only 17 years old his dream had come true!

'Ever since my first visit to Egypt... it had been my ambition to dig in the valley.'
Howard Carter

THE LORD AND THE LEGEND

To his great joy, Carter was eventually allowed to take part in excavations, known as digs. His work studying inscriptions led him to believe that the tomb of the legendary boy-king Tutankhamun lay hidden somewhere in the Valley of the Kings. And Carter was determined to find it.

The problem was that searching for tombs cost a great deal of money and Carter was not a rich man.

Luckily, an amateur Egyptologist called George Herbert, 5th Earl of Carnarvon, who was living in Egypt for his health, was enormously wealthy. He had funded several digs but lacked the knowledge needed to identify his finds, so he searched for a learned man to aid him. The man he chose was Howard Carter.

In 1914, Lord Carnarvon won permission to excavate the Valley of the Kings. This was what Carter had been waiting for! He believed with all his heart that Tutankhamun's tomb lay somewhere in the rocky cliffs of that ancient burial ground.

But work in the Valley would have to wait, because in the summer of 1914, the world went to war.

DIGGING UP DISAPPOINTMENT

Carter's excavations finally began in November 1917, and continued until the spring, when the heat of the Egyptian sun made the work impossible. No tomb was found that winter.

Work continued over the next four winters, but still no tombs were unearthed.

Everyone, including Lord Carnarvon, was losing hope that Tutankhamun's burial place would ever be found.

Everyone, that is, except Carter.

ONE LAST CHANCE

In the summer of 1922, Lord Carnarvon summoned Carter to his home at Highclere Castle in Hampshire. Carter dreaded the meeting. Years of costly digging had produced no results and he suspected that Carnarvon had finally lost patience. His deepest fears were confirmed. Lord Carnarvon would no longer fund the search for Tutankhamun.

However, Carter's belief was unwavering. He knew that pots, linen, seals and other artefacts bearing the name of Tutankhamun had been found near the area they were digging. The young pharaoh must be somewhere close! So certain was he that he offered to pay for the work himself and, if he was successful, to share the results with Carnarvon.

The two men studied the map which charted the five years of excavations. There was only one small area, beneath the remains of huts used by the builders of Rameses VI's tomb, that had yet to be explored. Lord Carnarvon was touched by Carter's passion and determination. He agreed to fund one last season.

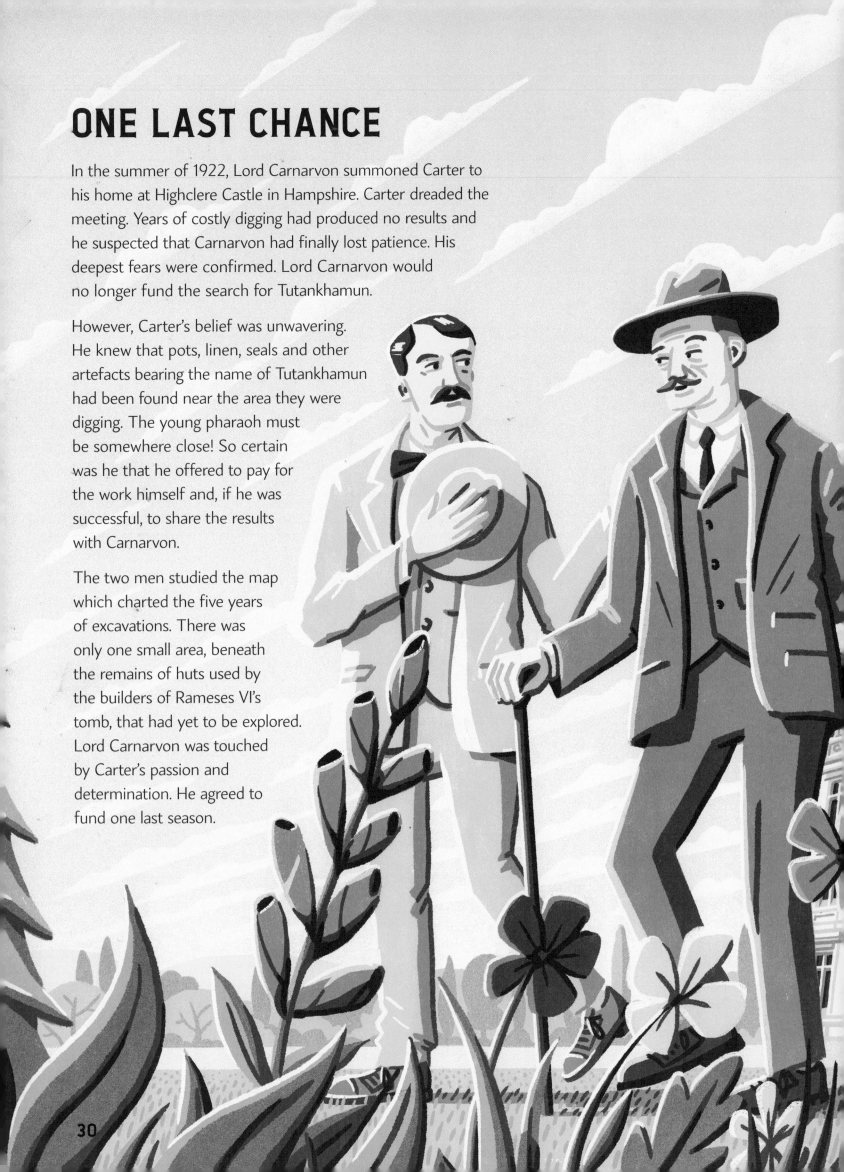

1922

'Season after season after season had drawn a blank; we had worked for months at a stretch and found nothing ... we had almost made up our minds that we were beaten.'

Howard Carter

A STEP INTO THE UNKNOWN

With the funds secured for one more year, Carter returned to Egypt. The search resumed on 1 November 1922.

The fierce heat of the desert sun made digging thirsty work. A young boy named Hussein Abdou-El-Rasoul, had been hired to bring water to relieve tired workers. On the morning of 4 November, Hussein arrived at the dig and brushed aside some sand to set down the heavy jars he was carrying. As he did so, his hand struck something hard. Hussein had discovered a step.

By the time the sun set the following day, 12 steps and the top of a doorway had been unearthed.

But Carter knew the discovery wasn't all his own. The very next morning he sent for Lord Carnarvon to join him from England.

'Anything, literally anything, might lie beyond that passage, and it needed all my self-control to keep from breaking down the doorway and investigating then and there.'

'At last have made wonderful discovery in Valley: a magnificent tomb with seals intact; re-covered same for your arrival; congratulations.'

Message sent from Howard Carter to Lord Carnarvon, 5 November 1922

THE DAY OF DAYS!

Three weeks after Howard Carter sent for Lord Carnarvon, the two men stood together in front of the tomb's entrance, hardly daring to breathe.

Carter lit a candle, then carefully chipped a hole in the doorway just large enough for him to see inside. Lord Carnarvon asked in a trembling voice, "Can you see anything?"

Carter finally replied...

The flickering candlelight revealed objects of breathtaking beauty –
and everywhere the glint of gold!

'The day of days, the most wonderful that I have ever lived through, and certainly one whose like I can never hope to see again.'

Howard Carter

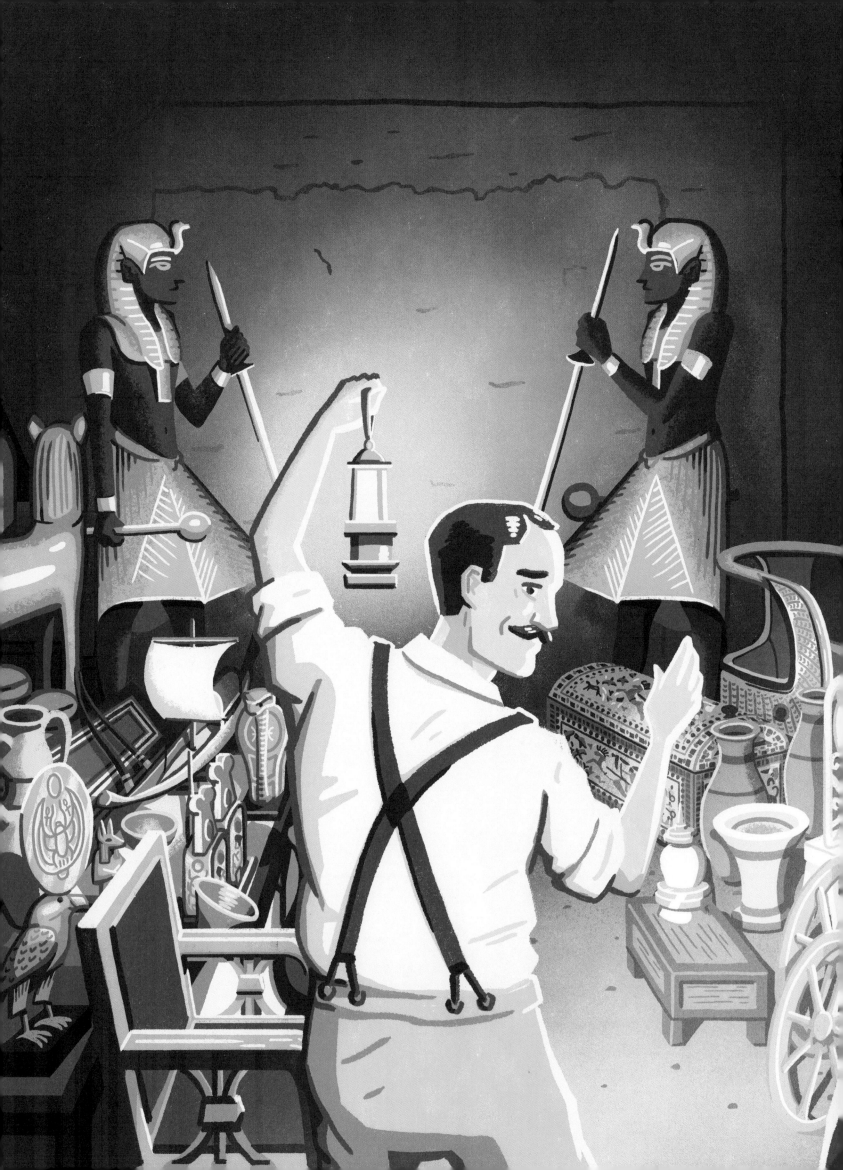

WONDERFUL THINGS

The hole was made larger and the two men entered the tomb. Everywhere they looked were treasures piled upon treasures, unseen by anyone for thousands of years.

There were golden couches, statues, ornate cups, and boxes and baskets filled with all the things a pharaoh would need in the afterlife. But there was one thing missing. Where was Tutankhamun?

There was a sealed entrance at the end of the room - was it possible that the young pharaoh lay beyond? As impatient as Carter was to explore further, he knew this would have to wait. Everything would need to be photographed and recorded, and the chamber cleared.

RNARVON
N INNER
S TOMB

h-Amen's
nspects
rvation.

PERTS

READ ALL ABOUT IT!

A few months later, in February 1923, an official opening was held. Chairs were set up for important guests who were waiting excitedly to see Howard Carter reveal what lay behind the sealed entrance. What appeared was a wall of shimmering gold – the side of a massive shrine! Carter had found the burial chamber of Tutankhamun.

News of the great discovery hit newspaper headlines around the world. But with few facts or photographs to fill their pages, journalists made up stories about a curse hidden in the tomb. No curse was ever found, but this didn't stop people believing it to be the cause of death of anyone connected with the tomb.

By October 1923, Carter and his team had removed the doors of the outer shrine to reveal a nest of three more shrines. The fourth contained a magnificent stone sarcophagus. Inside this was a coffin. Would this contain the pharaoh's mummy? The question would have to wait because, at that critical moment, a big argument about who would take charge of the burial chamber broke out between Carter and the Egyptian authorities.

Things were eventually settled in January 1925. Carter's team found two more coffins inside the first, the last of which was solid gold. On 28 October its lid was finally opened and the magnificent burial mask of Tutankhamun revealed.

The pharaoh's rest had been undisturbed for over 3,000 years... until now.

To
Dig
Des
Curs
of Eg

WHAT'S
INSIDE?

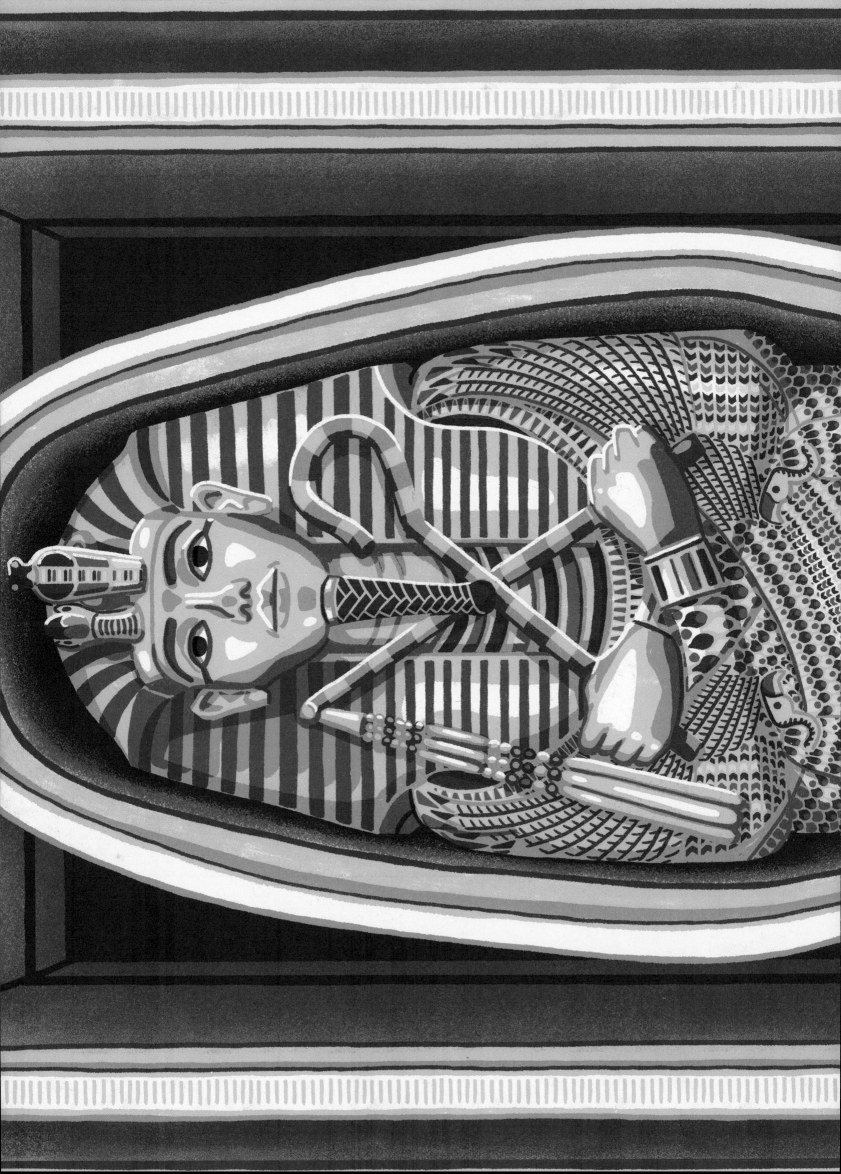

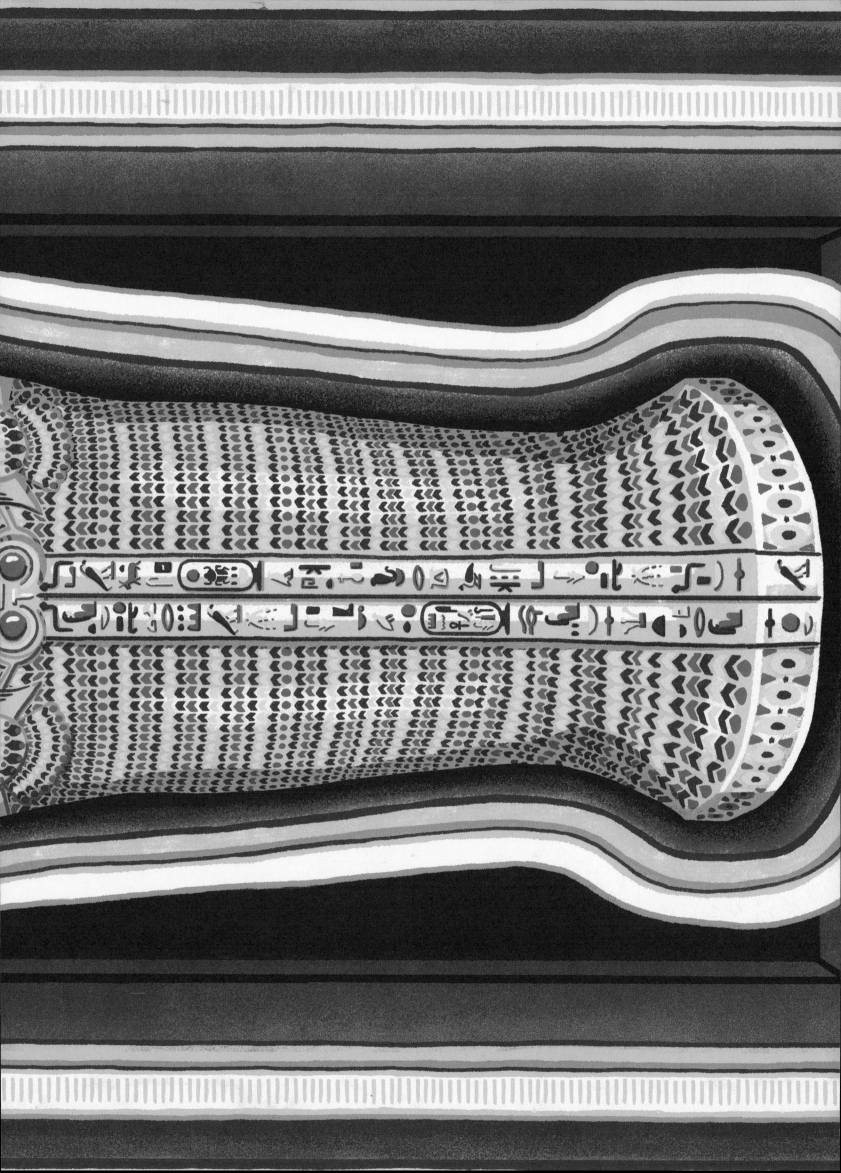

THE LEGEND LIVES ON

In total, Tutankhamun's tomb held more than 3,000 objects. Cataloguing and preserving each of these objects took Howard Carter and his team ten years.

After careful study, the mummy of the great pharaoh was returned to his tomb to resume his rest, deep within the Valley of the Kings in Egypt.

The Rosetta Stone, the key to discovering the secrets of ancient Egypt, can be seen in the British Museum in London, England.

Excavations continue to this day, and although no discoveries as legendary as that of the tomb of Tutankhamun have been unearthed since, many believe the Valley of the Kings still holds secrets beneath its shifting sands.

MASK

Found covering the head of Tutankhamun. Made from 10 kg of solid gold, brightly coloured glass and semi-precious stones.

The vulture and the cobra represent Upper and Lower Egypt. The cobra is ready to spit venom into the eyes of enemies of the pharaoh.

CANOPIC CHEST

Skilfully crafted from translucent stone.
Guarded by the images of four goddesses.
The chest holds four beautifully carved
jars containing the preserved organs
of the pharaoh.

WISHING CUP

Carved in the shape of a lotus blossom.
Found just inside the first chamber of the
tomb, dropped by one of the thieves.
It is inscribed with a wish for the
pharaoh's spirit.

After being removed, the treasures from the tomb of Tutankhamun
were taken to the Egyptian Museum in Cairo, where they can be seen
displayed in all their glittering glory.

KEY CHARACTERS

AKHENATEN

Pharaoh of Egypt 1353–1336 BCE. Moved the capital of the Egyptian kingdom to Amarna from Thebes and outlawed the worship of all the Egyptian gods except for Aten, god of the sun disk. Father of Tutankhaten (later Tutankhamun). Buried in Amarna and later moved to the Valley of the Kings.

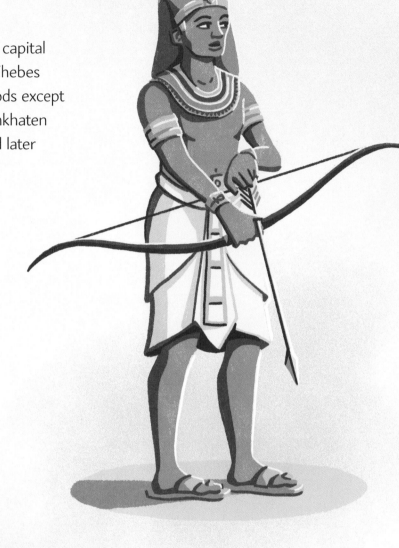

TUTANKHAMUN

Pharaoh of Egypt 1333–1323 BCE. Son of Akhenaten and one of his senior wives, Kiya. Returned the capital of Egypt to Thebes and resumed the worship of the traditional gods. Married to Ankhesenpaaten and died unexpectedly, aged 19, from unknown causes. Buried in the Valley of the Kings.

HOWARD CARTER
May 1874–March 1939

Born in London, Carter travelled to Egypt aged 17 to draw and copy the discoveries made there. After years of searching, he discovered the tomb of Tutankhamun in 1922. Howard Carter died in 1939, from natural causes, years after completing work on the tomb.

GEORGE HERBERT, 5TH EARL OF CARNARVON
June 1866–April 1923

Sponsor of Carter's excavations. Lord Carnarvon was injured in a car accident in 1901, which left him in poor health. He died from an infected mosquito bite before he could see inside the coffins of Tutankhamun. Many believe Carnarvon to be one of the first victims of 'the curse'.

HUSSEIN ABDOU-EL-RASOUL
Dates unknown

According to some sources, this was the name of a local Egyptian boy hired to carry water to the workers at the Valley of the Kings. Discovered the first step of the entrance to the tomb of Tutankhamun. Believed to be from the Abdou-El-Rasoul family, known for their ability to locate tombs.

THEODORE M. DAVIS
1837–February 1915

Retired American lawyer and sponsor of the excavations between 1902 and 1913. Davis was responsible for the discovery of nearly thirty tombs, although none were intact. Davis died before Carter's discovery of the tomb of Tutankhamun, believing there to be nothing left to find.

For my darlings Lily and Daisy – S.M.

For Isaac, Arty and Ted – J.W.L.

First published in Great Britain in 2018 by Wren & Rook

ISBN: 978 1 5263 6007 6
E-book ISBN: 978 1 5263 6062 5
10 9 8 7 6 5 4 3 2 1

Wren & Rook
An imprint of
Hachette Children's Group
Part of Hodder & Stoughton
Carmelite House
50 Victoria Embankment
London EC4Y 0DZ

An Hachette UK Company
www.hachette.co.uk
www.hachettechildrens.co.uk

Publishing Director: Debbie Foy
Editors: Corinne Lucas and Alice Horrocks
Art Director: Laura Hambleton
Designer: Lizzie Ballantyne

Printed in China